AMINA CHITEMBO

Multi-Award Winner. Author. Speaker. Trainer.
Productivity and Certified High-Performance Coach.

PROFITABLE TEAMS

How to Increase Productivity and Profits Through Coaching

www.aminachitembo.com

Disclaimer

This publication and its contents are provided for informational purposes only. All information and ideas are provided in good faith or in opinion of the author, and the author's research findings. To the best of the author's knowledge and experience the information is true and honest. The author, reserve the right to vary or change any such opinions subsequently.

The names of people in this book have been changed to protect their privacy.

Editing and Layout: Diverse Cultures Publishing

Cover Designed: Ahsan Chuhadry, Graphics Designer

Published by Diverse Cultures Publishing, UK.

Website: www.diverse-cultures.co.uk

Email address: publishing@diverse-cultures.co.uk

Postal Address: 28–29 Maxwell Road, Peterborough, PE2 7JE.

Paperback ISBN: 978-0-9957396-5-9.

Contents

To my late mum, Margaret Lelemba Chitembo.
The woman to taught me the value of hard work,
and to never settle for the ordinary.

Introduction

> *"Be a leader, coach and mentor not a microman-ager. Look after your staff, and they will give you 200%. Micromanage them, and it will cost you."*

In recent years, organisations have become more dynamic in the way they function. The landscape has moved, and the workplace that excels is one that is value driven, delivery focused and motivational to the most important asset, the people.

We all are seeking more than just a salary in a job; we want more f a challenge; we want to be seen and heard we want to be motivated and supported we want to be treated with respect, motivated and to be led to a high achievement standard.

In return, people are willing to give extra to the organisation because they are invested in it. A great workplace is a second home; great teammates are like a second family.

There is a lot to learn from the silicon valley community and other similar organisations around the world. Companies are making billions, with teams around the world working from home, in cafes or even on cruise ships.

Modern leaders are confident that they do not have to monitor and watch their teams with an eagle eye to ensure they are producing results. Results show up on the balance sheet. Trust and respect are a major part of a great working environment. People are given autonomy to act and be accountable for their days, which pays dividends to the `shareholders.

You the leader instill a culture of trust and ownership in your teams and they take personal responsibility for moving your business to exponential success.

But how do you achieve that amidst competing priorities?

The answer is in coaching. Whatever it is called and the context in which it is employed, there are many names attached to coaching;

- → Productivity coaching
- → Business coaching
- → High-performance coaching
- → Leadership coaching and the list goes on.

Investing in coaching not only allows you to teach your staff to answer their questions, but they become sophisticated, they build strong interpersonal skills, credibility, and confidence in their abilities, leading to delivery of successful and profitable outcomes. Through investing in coaching you improve the health environment for staff and people who use and buy your services.

You build '**Profitable Teams**'

CHAPTER ONE

Coaching Profitable Business Teams

Staff is the most valuable assets in any business regardless of where in the world your company is based. If the leadership can treat their staff with respect and as part of the professional family, they are on the winning path.

Coaching has become more widely used as a fundamental tool for great leaders who value their employees. The capability of dealing with the challenges leaders face in their roles of ensuring that their respective organisations are more competitive and profitable in the longer term, thus improving individual and organisational performance.

The value and benefits of coaching to an Organisation and its Individuals are slowly being accepted in the UK as well as other parts of the world.

Coaching is not just for the sports industry. It is vastly used in most of the developed countries, in the UK there appears to be a reluctance to invest in coaching for a start.

In my opinion, in the United Kingdom coaching seems to be reserved for top management or executives. I know that is a big claim. In my years of employment, and as a business coach that is what I have found, it is mostly a confidential 'thing' sometimes even mistaken for therapy.

In discussions with fellow coaches and with some of my coaching clients, there appears to be a level of stigma to receiving coaching.

Would you agree with my assertion?

I would love to hear your views on this, send me a message.

The Chartered Institute of Personnel and Development published report '*Coaching and buying coaching services* (CIPD, 2004)',. states that some factors have driven the increased use of coaching; included are:

- → ability to adapt to rapid change
- → organisational downsizing means newly promoted individuals requiring support
- → lifelong learning needs
- → costs associated with poor performance
- → senior level employees needing someone to confide in
- → personal responsibility for the development
- → The report states that HR/training practitioners almost universally believe;

"Coaching is an effective way of promoting learning; it can have an impact on the organisation's bottom line and can deliver tangible benefits to individuals and organisations."

The Learning Partnership Consultancy, in their white paper '*Building a business case for coaching*' (LPC, 2010), indicate that in recent years the value of coaching has become increasingly accepted and executive coaching is now widely used as a leadership development practice.

In a recent survey of 347 leaders, 40% of respondents reported that their organisation was doing more coaching in 2008 than 2007, whereas only 10% reported doing less. In their most recent 2010 survey, the CIPD found coaching was taking place in 83% of respondents' organisations. In the same CIPD survey, there was evidence that organisations are still spending on coaching despite the harsh economic conditions.

The study suggests that coaching is an essential tool for ensuring that leaders can deal with the challenges of their role within the pressures of the current economic climate.

However, as with any leadership growth tools, it is essential to ask the senior managers how successful the coaching is in improving individual and organisational performance within their organisation?

Many organisations have attempted to measure the return on investment (ROI) of coaching programmes in financial terms.

This book will guide you through the jungle of understanding the value and benefits of coaching and how great leaders use coaching to retain the most valuable asset for any winning organisation, their people. Gone are the days when 'James' and 'Shanna' stayed in the job until he was part of the fabric. If they do not feel the love, they leave or stick around only giving the bare minimum. Both scenarios come at a massive cost to the business.

'Profitable Teams' book explores how companies adopt coaching as productivity and motivational tool

for improving individual, team, and organisational performance leading to an increase in profitability

The values and benefits of coaching to the organisation and the people within the organisation;

The differences in the potential outcomes between an organisation that adopts a coaching approach and the one that does not;

The advantages and disadvantages of using coaching as opposed to other tools such as mentoring or consultancy

The difference between coaching and mentoring or consultancy

How a coach can measure the value they bring to the organisation and its individuals;

The process involved in the Coach/Client dialogue with samples of Coach/Client dialogue.

Influencing Consistently High Performance

"Coaching is a process that enables learning and development to occur and thus performance to improve" -Parsole.

Coaches are called upon when people want to increase their productivity or when someone wants to perform at a higher level than where they are. Most organisations will bring in a consultant when there is a crisis. I have worked in organisations as a consultant, and most of the time the staff are not happy having a consultant around for many reasons.

The biggest being that obviously the consultant is seen as an outsider who comes in to change how we do things and get paid a lot of money. But what if organisations made sure that their employees are developed within the organisation and given the support and coaching that would empower them to do more. To worker harder and perform at a heightened level consistently and be ready to jump into new projects with enthusiasm and the willingness to take ownership.

Companies can benefit more by retaining happy and high performing staff. Most of my clients want to leave a job because they don't feel like it meets their needs, they want a challenge, or they get passed by and feel that their contribution to the organisation is not appreciated. In 2017 I had the opportunity of coaching a director of a multimillion company private company. I will call him James.

James had built his company from the bottom up. While the company was small, he was always talking to his employees had a visible presence. As the company grew and the demand on his time increased, naturally he employed more people to his leadership team to help him run the business. The business was now in Seven Cities around the UK, and it was churning out money until one year, the financial situation looked different.

That was not the only problem with the company. There was suddenly a low staff retention rate and a high number of sickness absence.

The first thought for James was to call all his directors to an emergency meeting. After deliberations back and forth it came to light that there was negative energy in the organisation. The company had become a money churning machine which had lost the appreciation of the people that were in the forefront of that success. These are his words, not mine.

His first reaction was anger and frustration. He was disappointed in himself. However, this is not something he wanted to show at work.

This happens when someone reaches the level they wanted to get to?

There are many different types of coaches. Coaching is used in many different professions to help people reach high levels of productivity in their given career. You have heard of sports coaches, voice coaches, career coaches, and the list goes on. Many thought leaders have described coaching in different ways. He decided to hire a coach, but not just any coach, he wanted a coach that would help him turn things around and keep him consistent. Before I continue with this story, I want to check how clear we are about some of the words we use.

Who is a coach and what can they do for you?

Who is a coach? Several authors and thought leaders described coaching in different ways. However, all the definitions have these key elements; Sir John Whitmore the author of Coaching for Performance describes coaching as 'Unlocking a person's potential to maximize his or her performance.'

Anthony G Grant in the international coaching federation presentation described coaching as 'A collaborative solution focussed, results-oriented, and systematic process in which the coach facilitates the enhancement work performance, life experience, self-directed learning and personal growth.'

Other authors have stated that to be successful; a coach requires knowledge and understanding of the process of coaching as well as the variety of styles, skills, and techniques that are appropriate to the context in which the coaching takes place. A coach does not need to be an expert in their client's profession. What I have found though, both as a coach and a client myself is that it helps if the coach can include passion and humour in their toolkit. These two elements help the client relax and free to explore their wild goals and ideas, which is where most productivity comes from.

Coaching is paying attention to the client, in both what they are saying and what they are 'not saying,' feeding back what the coach has heard, and then asking questions to encourage fresh thinking and mind unlocking from the client, and facilitating, growth in the whole person. This generally brings happiness and better mental health and wellbeing. A person who is happy is generally more productive and a pleasure to be around. Coaching brings about personal reflection, learning and development leading to a commitment to self-directive problem solving and decision making.

Organisations that invest in coaching for their workforce achieve better timelines and can retain key expert staff. Coaching is most often used to help leaders enhance their performance, and thereby elevating the performance of the organisation. Organisations often face the challenge of developing greater confidence, initiative, and problem-solving capabilities among their staff.

Organisations need staff at all levels to be more self-sufficient, resourceful, creative and autonomous. This behaviour enables staff to operate at the higher strategic level, which makes their organisations more productive and competitive. It is what all organisations strive to achieve.

Below are some of the benefits of coaching in organisations according to a reliable source; Results You Get with Executive Coaching http://www.monarch-janus.com/mja-executive-coaching-results.html:

→ improved engagement and retention of key talent
→ stronger talent conduit for better future planning
→ increased enablement and ownership of personal and career development

→ enhanced leadership capability and presence

→ faster and smoother transitions into new roles

→ improved communication and relationships with the principal stakeholders

→ greater alignment between leaders' goals and organisational objectives

→ better use of strengths to improve performance

→ increased awareness of development opportunities and to address them

→ improved people management skills

→ more balance between work and life priorities

→ better prepared to manage through organisational change and transition

→ enhanced individual and team productivity

There are many developmental tools available to leaders, and their staff. Coaching is one of them and possibly the most overlooked. Learning and development are fundamental to the better performance of an organisation.

Coaching is a developmental resource that can build expert teams if incorporated into their staff development strategy.

"Coaching has high potential to enable individuals to develop competencies, such as leadership and behavioural skills directly related to enriched performance and business results."

Coaching can help you to get comfortable with giving more power to employees through delegation and training. You then get to enjoy that holiday you have been putting off because of deadlines.

For as aspiring business coach, there is increasing potential in the marketplace for coaches; organisations are constantly looking for ways to retain hardworking individuals and help them to become even more independent.

People can gain more confidence and become extra-ordinary by learning high-performance skills through coaching. In his book: *'High-Performance Habits: How extra-ordinary people become that way,'* Brendon Burchard *shares the results of intensive research conducted by him and a team of researchers from various universities in the USA. The research results show* **six behaviours of high performers which can be learned by anyone. These** behaviours are:

→ **Clarity** – People who seek clarity tend to get better results. They know where they are going.

→ **Energy** – if you can maintain high levels of energy they are likely to achieve.

→ **Courage** – Courage allows people to think outside the box try ways that will give better results.

→ **Productivity** – This is a big one for many of us, with so many disturbances, learning how to keep your day productive, prioritization, quick wins, less talk more action, lean working, if you can horn these skills, you are on to a winner.

→ **Necessity** – all to do with the why, or the need, we all need a reason to do what we must do. Some of those reasons can be what separates the high-performers to non-performers. High-performers tend to have a high need for success.

→ **Influence** – People who can find ways to influence others will always get more. Influence used correctly can lead to great results.

→ **Persuasion** – The ability to get through a difficult deal requires a level of persuasion. If a salesperson can persuade a customer to give their credit card details to buy the product a company is selling, or if one can persuade a client to close that deal, the leader will be smiling, right?

Imagine the exponential growth in your organisation, when everyone becomes aware of the power that is a high performer brings. Some clients I have worked with have decided to embed high-performance habits in their life, and the results have been tremendous. All skills can be learned.

"All Habits can be learned and unlearned."

People can be coached in these high-performance habits. A coach is a non-judgemental professional who you can happily speak to without feeling silly about your big and crazy goals.

According to the 2013 Executive Coaching Survey by Stanford University and the Miles Group found that two-thirds of the 200 CEOs they surveyed reported having no outside advice on their leadership skills, but they were very receptive to making leadership changes style in response to coaching.

Another piece of research carried out by the Coaching Academy, UK revealed fascinating findings with the top five skills of desired development for executives and leadership teams:

→ Conflict Resolution
→ Coaching and Mentoring
→ Delegation
→ Listening
→ Planning

These soft skills plus motivation and interpersonal skills have an important place in the leader's daily life. They allow leaders to lose the 'boss' syndrome of always telling people what to do. Instead, they help to build a culture where their management team can also motivate and inspire staff.

Eric Schmidt, a chief executive officer of Google, one of the largest and most successful companies in the world has stated that the secret to his business success has a coach.

Can Coaching Improve Performance?

Yes, it can. Think about the world's greatest performers; athletes, musicians, and football teams, they all use coaches, and they invest time and money in the best coaches for their trade. I once had an opportunity to train and be coached by a man in the USA called Roger Love.

You may not know who this person is, nonetheless, he is responsible for coaching some of the most famous people in the world. Roger has helped Oscar, Screen actors' guild and dozens of Grammy award winners with voice coaching, people like Michael Jackson, Tyra Banks, Tony Robbins, Selina Gomez, the cast of Glee or if you are in the boomers, generation you may know people like Jeff Bridges and many more.

If coaching were not *'a thing,'* if it did not work, people like me would not be in a job. I get new client inquiries all the time to my coaching practice, and at times I cannot take everyone that asks me to coach them.

For those that I get to work with, the results are remarkable. Unlike therapy, people come to coaching because they have tried on their own and they have gained a level of success, but they know that they could do better and they need that extra help to be the best version of themselves.

Coaching provides fast and positive results, which is attributed to participative nature of the coaching environment. The client or person being coached is encouraged to dig deep into their mind to find solutions and see things from a different perspective.

Coaching is very person-centered and focuses on the client and their problem. The aim is always to attain the best result that is going to help the person being coached to achieve their goals. Through achievement of goals, morale and general wellbeing are improved.

Coaching can take place over an extended period spreading the overall welfare, which means the client will constantly be held to account for achieving the results and encouraged to work on issues that need improvement.

A great coaching experience often leads to improvement in performance; this can be; meeting targets and goals, improving performance, reducing absence, even creating healthy competition in the workplace. Employees are more open to personal learning and development because coaching does not feel like training which will be packed and forgotten the following day.

Coaching increases the ability to identify solutions to specific work-related issues and achieve greater ownership, responsibility and develop better self-awareness. For employees who feel they need improvement of specific skills or behaviour or greater clarity in roles and objectives, coaching can offer quick, usable solutions.

Coaching can help leaders engage fuller with the individual's talents and potential. It can demonstrate a commitment to employees leading to a healthy and happy workforce who will be key in increasing the organisational productivity.

Coaching can help the implementation of a new culture, which has great potential to improve relationships between people and teams, especially within integrated teams, mergers, and takeovers.

Coaching has the potential to improve the mental health and wellbeing within the workplace, leading to increase morale, general happiness, and staff retention.

"Happy teams offer 200% effort to the organisation, thus increasing productivity and sustainability."

Performance Coaching Scenario

Jane is Tina's manager. Tina has been turning up at work late and seems to be absent-minded and increasingly missing deadlines. A one to one meeting is set up for Jane and Tina.

Tina recognises her problem but does not think it is necessary to share it at work. She is worried about losing her job, so this meeting makes her visibly anxious. In the meeting the conversation goes as follows:

Jane: *"Thanks for coming in Tina, you look a bit tired would you like a cup of tea. Let us go and grab a tea and then we will continue."*

This takes them 10 minutes but helps Tina to relax and less pressured as they commence the meeting. Now the dialogue begins

Jane: *"How are things, Tina?"*

Tina: *"Hmmm things are okay, thanks, I am fine."*

Jane: *"I have called this meeting to see if there is a way we can explore a few issues and improve the slipping deadlines."*

Tina: *"Oh, I am sorry, I will improve, I promise."*

Jane: *"No, that is not an issue for me as such. I want to see if something is going on that is causing the problems, I am sure if we can deal with the source of the problem then the rest will be easy (with a smile) what do you think?"*

Tina: *"I guess so . . .(silence)."*

Jane: *"How about we talk about any areas you are currently struggling with?"* (Silence, Jane mirroring Tina's position and maintaining eye contact.)

Tina (after a pause): *"I guess I have been struggling to come on time because my mum is not very well. She is living with me; I must fend for her in the morning while I wait for my sister to arrive to take over. This means I end up leaving late and get caught up in traffic. It also worries me that on Mondays and Thursdays there is no one to look after her, so I have to keep phoning to check in on her."*

Jane: *"Okay, I am sorry to hear about your mum, that is a very valid reason."*

Jane goes on to ask several questions to understand the situation better, allowing Tina to express herself without interruptions freely.

In the end, Jane asks: *"Tina, is there anything we could do to make things easier?"*

Tina now feels listened to; she is happier and able to think through solutions. Together, Tina and Jane explore a few of Tina's suggestions with the aim of finding a win-win solution. They come up with solutions that suit both Tina and the company.

They agree to review the situation monthly.

Soon Tina's performance picks up as she feels part of the solution to increase the performance and at the same time feels that Jane understands her. Jane values Tina's contribution and has helped her make adaptations that have resulted in higher productivity and getting them back on track in meeting their targets.

CHAPTER TWO

Demonstrating Value of Coaching

"Measuring the influence of coaching can validate the value and return on investment."

—Amina Chitembo

As with any other aspect of the business, it is also important to for accountability, to demonstrate what the staff is achieving from the coaching. This will help to plan future action. Creating culture coaching is not easy, but the measures set out in this chapter will help you to evaluate success and measure the value that the coaching is bringing to your business.

Consulting with staff – It is a two-way street, coaching is more likely to be accepted if your staff feel party to it. It is not just something they are told to do. Any effective coaching programme must have a beginning and an end. It must also have a clear structure and expected outcomes must be set. Coaching that has no end becomes a pointless 'friendship,' financial drain, and can lead to dependency.

Records must be kept as this can help in several ways including calculating the value, lessons learned. The record is not a record of the actual coaching; it is a summary of the requirements and results. The actual coaching is confidential between the coach and the coaching client.

The best times to carry out a consultation are:

Before the coaching is suggested, to identify the needs and decide the most appropriate type of coaching.

At the beginning of the coaching programme, to set out a starting level.

At the middle point of the coaching programme; to help assess progress and help make necessary adjustments if required.

At the end of the coaching programme. To review the coaching result against the need recorded at the beginning and the previous stages.

These results can be analysed and give a clear picture of the impact and value the coaching has had. The consultation does not need to be complicated. It would aim to understand what the employee and their line manager feel have changed at the end and what work still needs to be carried out.

Review Monitoring Data - Reviewing the data from some staff that has gone through the coaching process will help the leadership incorporate the learning into the wider organisation.

Analysing the records collated from monitoring on an annual basis will help you measure progress and prompt. A simple system of electronically recording can be adopted; this can be in the form of an excel spreadsheet that can be analysed or a survey programme such as survey monkey or google forms. Even with the simple versions of this data can help the organisation immensely.

Challenges of Measuring Value

There can be challenges in measuring the value that coaching has brought in that employee might feel pressured to say it worked. The results of measuring the value of coaching can vary greatly. It can be very difficult to understand or measure the difference

The following actions might help management to mitigate the challenges of measurement of value to the organisation. The organisation can also help other organisations by publishing these results. The more data is made available by companies the more they are likely to attract the right employees and that could make the difference.

→ Make the surveys or measurement anonymous
→ Make the questions fun
→ Use milestones
→ Under promise and over deliver
→ Adjust expectations
→ Clarify ownership
→ Clarify and improve incentives
→ Consider piloting
→ Incentivise reporting.

CHAPTER THREE

What Type of Coaching is Right?

"Each person holds so much power within themselves that needs to be let out. Sometimes they just need a little nudge, a little direction, a little support, a little coaching, and the greatest things can happen with the right coach."
—Pete Carroll, American Coach.

There are many different types of coaching that can be incorporated into an organisation. The benefits of coaching are dependent on the coaching needs of the organisation and the experience of the coach contracted to provide the coaching. Different types of coaching can help an organisation in various situations. Some of the ways an organisation can use the coaching are as follows:

Leadership Development Coaching

Leadership Development Coaching is a valuable type of coaching focused on build skills needed for leadership roles. This type of coaching can be used for people who are being primed to move into a leadership position, such as team leaders, graduate apprentices, and middle to senior management.

It helps them to become more effective leaders of their teams or coaching can be used to deal with issues such as conflict, motivation, and change. It would typically cover areas such as delegation skills, mentoring, team management, conflict resolution and confidence building. The focus is preparation for the client to perform at a higher position than they are currently.

High-Performance Coaching

This a new advanced and science-backed type of coaching introduced by the High-Performance Institute in the United States of America.

It aims at helping the client learn and incorporate high-performance habits into their daily life which will result in them performing at a consistently high level over the long term.

A 'Certified High-Performance Coach' helps the client to build discipline habits in core areas of life; clarity, energy, productivity, purpose, courage, and influence. It follows a curriculum that is future-oriented, ensuring that each coaching session within a cycle of twelve modules has specific outcomes and further activities for the client to practice in their own time. It is not an exam nor does the client need to report back to the coach.

High-Performance Coaching is advanced and is mainly suited to those who are high achievers and can take responsibility for their advancement and future. By intentionally building key practices in daily life both professional and personal, the client builds resilience and high levels of positivity and wellbeing which lead to higher **productivity** and **profitability.**

For full disclosure, I am a Certified High-Performance Coach, the rigorous training, and coaching from fellow high-performance coaches has helped me, leave my job, start a new business which is doing very well and write three books in within fifteen months. I have developed habits that help me to be more present with my family, my clients and business associates. I have learned to give myself time to re-energise throughout my day, to manage my stress levels and to do that one thing I dreaded doing all my life; selling.

Productivity Coaching

As a corporate and executive accredited coach, I also offer my clients a version of this coaching as **productivity coaching.** Productivity is more than just a set of tasks, targets and key performance indicators. It is the bloodline of every human being, both in personal and professional life. Think of those days when you do not feel like leaving your bed, the house, nonetheless you must get up and move your energy levels.

Your mind is not just in it. You reach the office, and you get busy, attend several meetings, phone calls, chat with colleagues, and before you know it, it is time to go home. On your commute, upon reflection, you realise that the day has gone by and your to-do list is still full.

You have not moved any closer to complete that proposal which will win you the next contract. Frustration sets in, when you get home, you try to catch up, the family needs you. You give them a couple of hours, but your mind is not fully there because all you can think about is the work that you must finish.

What, is there was another way? You wake up with intention and do everything in your day purposefully minding all the triggers and unproductive tendencies. You deal with them accordingly because now you have learned your high-performance habits. You know which habit to employ at the right time until it becomes part of your life. That is what high-performance coaching is all about.

Transformational Coaching

This type of coaching is mainly required in time of large-scale transformation and redesign. Some organisational change, such as downsizing and takeovers, can develop into a rapidly evolving environment where leaders must constantly anticipate and quickly respond to any eventualities that come with the change process.

Transformational coaching is critical in helping key employees acquire the appropriate skills to deal with consequences such as staff movement, discontentment, leaving, and any anxieties which if not resolved adequately, will lead to undesired consequences.

If an organisation develops a culture in which employees are coached and supported by change, key decisions, style of implementing a change might be received positively. The employees are more likely to commit themselves to this proposed change.

Team Effectiveness Coaching

Is used to maximise the effectiveness of a team, at any level. It seeks to eliminate personal and political issues from company objectives to foster high-performing teams. Team coaching is useful for executives, managers, and team leaders as well as other people who require a range of common skills to perform their duties.

Conflict Resolution or Conciliation Coaching

Is focussed on resolving conflicts and to prevent escalation of a conflict situation within teams or in leaders who need to work together but do not seem to get along. Conflict in organisations is inevitable; it is a healthy part of life, people express their passion in different ways.

If left unresolved, conflicts can cause disputes and disruption to productivity ultimately affecting profitability. Conflict Resolution coaching can be offered to individuals or groups; it can help the staff to focus on the work as opposed to concentrating on the personalities.

Here are some of the areas where a great coach will help leaders and their organisations:

→ identify team strengths and development needs
→ Create organisational strategies with action plans and accountability to help employees stay on track
→ adopt and reinforce executive leadership competencies crucial to the organisation's culture
→ Positive and sustainable transformational change
→ Develop skills and practices, learn coaching skills they can implement
→ Enhanced career planning and development with an action-oriented plan
→ Create greater work/life balance

Coaching, Mentoring or Consultancy

"The purpose of coaching is to instil intensity to critical thinking. The purpose of Consulting is to seek the help of a critical thinker to educate or do what one cannot do. The purpose of mentoring is somewhere between the coaching and consulting. The outcome of all three is true edification."

—Amina Chitembo

What is the Difference?

Coaching and mentoring are both processes that enable individuals to achieve their full potential. Coaching and mentoring share many similarities as well as differences.

Let us get consultancy out of the way. Many times, I am contacted by a client or an organisation requiring my services. They start off by saying they want to coach which sometimes they call mentoring and then as we discuss their requirements it becomes apparent that they are more in need of consultancy.

Consultancy

To break it down to the best of my ability in explaining based on my mini research. I will tackle consultancy first and then go on to compare the other two.

Consultancy is more concerned with giving advice and mostly undertaken by subject matter experts. It focuses on advising the organisation or specific members staff. In most cases to leaders or project teams. Most consultants are experts in a field.

The consultants usually advise the businesses what to do to improve productivity, or in some cases, they will do it for them and charge a lot of money for it. The health service in the UK has been in the spotlight for spending lots of money on consultants or interim coverage for crucial gaps in provision. I do have an opinion on that, but I will leave it for another book.

Consultants respond to problems or fill in gaps in expertise. They ask questions that lead them to find the best way of solving the problem; they answer questions with advice that will help the business. They help you go from non-productive or failing to highly productive expeditiously.

They can play the role of the fixer. They will ask to gain clarity on the problem at hand; then they will provide a solution. They show you how to do something better, how to fix something, how to be successful, the consultant must possess knowledge and experience in the field that the client services.

Often, when I go into a public-sector organisation, it is to provide consultancy in my areas of expertise. It could be around commissioning, project management or contract management within community services. These interim leadership roles, where they need a specific problem solved swiftly without having to employ someone on a permanent basis.

Consulting is a process where the consultant instructs the client step by step on how to accomplish a specific goal or task that the consultant has already mastered. My uncle once told my ex-husband who tended reporting every little wrong thing I did that he will charge him consultancy for helping him step by step on how to run our home. I know this is so random, but it is true. So, I will run with it as a simplistic example.

Coaching Vs. Mentoring

The table below outlines some of the differences and similarities of coaching:

Coaching	Mentoring
Coaching is task oriented. The focus is on concrete issues, such as managing more effectively, speaking more articulately, and learning how to think strategically. It requires a content expert (coach) who can teach the client how to develop these skills on their own.	**Mentoring is relationship oriented.** It seeks to provide a safe environment where the mentor shares whatever issues affect his or her professional and personal success. Although one can use specific learning goals or competencies as a basis for creating the relationship, its focus goes beyond these areas to include things, such as work/life balance, self-confidence, self-perception, and how the personal influences the professional.
Coaching is short term. A coach can successfully be involved with a client for a short period,	**Mentoring is always long term.** Mentoring, to be successful, requires time in which both partners can

(Continue)

Coaching	Mentoring
maybe even just a few sessions. The coaching lasts for as long as is needed, depending on the purpose of the coaching relationship.	learn about one another and build a climate of trust that creates an environment in which the person receiving mentoring feels comfortable to share the real issues impacting on them and their success. Successful mentoring relationships can last for years.
Coaching is performance driven. The purpose of coaching is to improve the individual's performance on the job. It involves either enhancing current skills or acquiring new skills. Once the client successfully acquires the skills, the coach is no longer needed.	**Mentoring is development driven.** Its purpose is to develop the individual not only for the current job but also for the future. This distinction differentiates the role of the immediate manager and that of the mentor. It also reduces the possibility of creating conflict between the employee's manager and the mentor.

Coaching	Mentoring
Coaching does not require design. Coaching can be conducted almost immediately on any given topic. If a company seeks to provide coaching to a large group of individuals, the amount of design is involved in determining the competency area, expertise needed, and assessment tools used, but this does not necessarily require a long lead-time to implement the coaching program.	**Mentoring requires a design phase** to determine the strategic purpose for mentoring, the focus areas of the relationship, the specific mentoring models, and the specific components that will guide the relationship, especially the matching process.
The coachee's immediate manager is a critical partner in coaching. The manager often provides the coach with feedback on areas in which his or her employee is in need of coaching. This coach uses this information to guide the coaching process	**In mentoring, the immediate manager is indirectly involved.** Although they could offer suggestions to the employee on how to best use their new mentoring knowledge or may recommend to the matching committee on what would constitute a

(Continue)

Coaching	Mentoring
	good match, the manager often has no link to the mentor, and they do not communicate at all during the mentoring relationship. It helps maintain the mentoring relationship's integrity.

When to Consider Coaching

→ When a company is seeking to develop its staff in specific skills using performance management tools and involving the immediate manager

→ When a company has talented employees who are not meeting expectations

→ When a company is introducing change

→ When a company needs increased competency in specific areas

→ When a leader or executive needs assistance in acquiring a new skill as an additional responsibility

When to Consider Mentoring

→ When a company is seeking to develop its leaders or talent pool as part of succession planning

→ When a company seeks to develop its diverse employees to remove barriers, that hinder their success

→ When a company seeks to completely develop its employees in ways that are added to the acquisition of specific skills/competencies

→ When a company seeks to retain its internal expertise and experience residing in its baby boomer employees for future generations

→ When a company wants to create a workforce that balances the professional and the personal

When to Consider Consultancy

→ When an organisation is going through change and require expert advice

→ When there is shortage of staff and the organisation requires someone, who can fill a specific role immediately

A good coach will need to explain to potential clients what the difference is, they may also look at some similarities to put things into perspective. Below is an outline of some similarities in coaching and mentoring which differentiate them from consulting. Both coaching and mentoring:

→ Facilitate the exploration of needs, motivations, desires, skills and thought processes to assist the individual in making real, lasting change.

Use questioning techniques to facilitate client's thought processes to identify solutions and actions rather than take a wholly directive approach

→ Support the client in setting appropriate goals and methods of assessing progress about the goals

→ Observe, listen and ask questions to understand the client's situation

→ Creatively apply tools and techniques which may include one-to-one training, facilitating, counseling and networking.

→ Encouraging commitment to action and the development of lasting personal growth and change.

→ Maintain constructive regard for clients. It means that the coach is at all times supportive and non-judgemental of the client, and their lifestyle and aspirations.

→ Ensure that clients develop personal competencies and do not develop unhealthy dependencies on the coaching or mentoring relationship.

→ Evaluate the outcomes of the process, using objective measures wherever possible to ensure the relationship is successful, and the client is achieving their personal goals.

→ Encouraging the clients to improve competencies continually and to develop new developmental alliances where necessary to achieve their goals.

→ Work within their area of personal competence.

→ Possess qualifications and experience in the areas offering the skills-transfer coaching. Manage the relationship to ensure the client receives the appropriate level of service, and that programmes are neither too short nor too long.

Coaching, however, is a process facilitated by an appropriately qualified person who may not necessarily be an expert in the particular client's field. It follows a very specific process that helps the client discover much of the solution themselves. It builds confidence, a deeper level of competence and capability in problem-solving when they meet related problems in the future.

Consultants teach people or offer expert advice. A great consultant can teach the client some exciting techniques or skills to achieve a goal, but if the client wants to learn how to become successful, then they seek a qualified coach.

Why Coaching is a Winner

"To excel at the highest level - or any level, really - you need to believe in yourself, and hands down, one of the biggest contributors to my self-confidence has been private coaching."
—Stephen Curry

You can go so far alone, but you certainly need the help of a coach to get further faster. The best thing is to understand what coaching is and what other tools, you need that will help deliver results. Coaching is not about getting advice; it is about someone who you develop a personal relationship with, who is not your boss, colleague or someone who will not be afraid of calling you out on your incapacities or procrastination tendencies.

To understand the advantages and disadvantages of using coaching; as opposed to other tools such as mentoring or consultancy; This chapter looks at some advantages and disadvantages.

Advantages

Quick and tangible results - Coaching provides quick results, greater productivity, faster promotions, and has the potential to bring out the ideas the person did not know they possessed. Mentoring is dependent on the mentor's experience and capacity.

Coaching can focus on where the person needs to improve and involves high accountability to achieve the set goals which can be easy to see in a short time. Coaching provides clarity on values and what the person stands for, which leads to a greater conviction. A coach can use their skills and the goals management set to develop a plan, while the mentor may follow management set objectives without much lead way.

Precision - Coaching is time-limited, and most formal, i.e., provides set time for coaching sessions which gives the opportunity for faster action with greater precision. Mentoring is more informal and can achieve results but over a longer period.

Matching - most people will use a coach that they choose because they feel they are a match. There is a signed contract, and if either party wishes to break the relationship, there is no lasting damage. A possible disadvantage with a mentor-mentee relationship can be forced, such as when a supervisor assigns an experienced employee to tutor a new employee and the two don't get along.

The mentor may feel that they are unable to fulfill the role or the mentee may feel intimidated but will feel unable to refuse the offer, which can lead to a strained relationship.

Disadvantages

Cost – a coach costs more which can be a disadvantage. A coach mostly qualified professional and usually cost money whether indirect by the company paying for someone to be trained as a coach to provide coaching to colleagues or by hiring an external coach into the organisation.

The same is the case with a consultant. A mentor, on the other hand, does not need to have a mentoring qualification. It can be an experienced member of staff or colleague who passes on her knowledge and expertise to a less experienced member of the team. In some cases, a mentor is assigned by senior management as part of personal/professional development for the experienced colleague to move into a higher role or for the person they are mentoring.

Coaching out – Coaching is person-centred, and the result of the coaching could mean the coaching client realises that they are in the wrong job. They can move on, which can be seen as a disadvantage for the management because they can incur the cost of replacing the person in addition to paying for the coaching itself. Mentoring and Consultancy both are aimed at using the skills within the organisation as there are low chances that the person receiving the support will leave as a result.

CHAPTER FIVE

Coach and Client Dialogue

"Change will not come if we wait for some other person or some other time. We are the ones we've been waiting for. We are the change that we seek."
—Barack Obama

The coach-client dialogue should be one that has mutual respect, and it should follow a certain pattern for it to be non-directive. A coach needs to ask questions that reflect active listening skills.

A coach needs to provide a challenge for their client. They should ensure that they explain with clarity what the main points of the coaching relationship are. The contract should be fair and clear.

It is important to get the client to complete an intake questionnaire and to ask the client if there is anything that the coach needs to be aware of, that may affect the achievements of their goals, which could be communication or in some cases health. For example, if the client is due an operation at the time, they are saying they want to achieve the goal.

They may not remember to mention it, but a question in an intake questionnaire might work as a prompt for them to take into account that commitment as they come to the coaching, that way the coach and client can work around the issue and find a way of achieving the goal or allow extra time.

Assessing the client's position and maintain professionalism and compassion and ensuring that the coach-client boundaries are explained and monitored. Professional integrity is key to a successful relationship. A coach is sensitive to the ideas and must not seem shocked even if they feel the goal is unachievable.

The role of the coach is to help the client think through their goal and come up with achievable options and making sure they ask open-ended questions that the client will think through the plans without suggestions from the coach. Below are some of the key points the coach might want to cover to enable them to understand the client better.

Contracting: Key Points to Cover

With Manager	With Client
→ What is your perception of coaching?	→ Reasons for coaching
→ What outcomes are you seeking?	→ What are the client's leadership goals, aspirations?
→ How will they know when they are successful?	→ How will they know when they are successful?
→ Is the direct report a willing participant?	→ What success factors are important to your boss, direct reports, and peers?
→ How will the manager communicate this conversation to their direct report?	→ Challenges
	→ How often shall we meet?
→ How involved does manager want to be in the coaching process?	→ How will coach and client know that we are both on track?
	→ Cancellation policy
→ Confidentiality	→ Confidentiality

Source: Coaching for Results

CHAPTER SIX

Sample Coach and Client Dialogue

Below is a transcript of a coach/client session. It follows the GROW model from the book 'Coaching for Performance: The principles of and practice of coaching and leadership' 5th Edition by Sir John Whitmore. This is based on a true coaching conversation used by permission with one of my clients. The names have been changed to protect their confidentiality, and the session has been truncated to keep it short.

Client Profile

Meet Marcia, she is an Executive Director of Transformation in the National Health Service which is going through a difficult financial time, and she provides the much-needed turnaround for the business. She lives in Surrey. She is 43 years old, and she is married with three (3), teenage children.

Marcia holds a master's degree. She rose to her position as Director of Transformation and Redesign within four years of joining the public sector. Before that, she was a CEO of a small business, where she managed a small team of staff but had much wider reach regarding stakeholders.

The Issue: Her company is underperforming, and she is under pressure from her chief executive and governing body to deliver a business turnaround strategic plan and to implement it so that the organisation does not go into special measures.

The session is 60 minutes of which 10 minutes is introduction and housekeeping, leaving a full 50 minutes for the session. Below is a transcript of the 50 minutes session.

Greeting	**Coach**	Good morning Marcia, how are you today?
	Client	Good morning Amina, I am well thanks, how are you?
	Coach	I am well thanks, is there anything you wish to ask me before we start the session today? No, I am ready, if anything comes up along the way I will ask
Intro	**Coach**	Fabulous, let's begin, today's session will be the same as the last two sessions, it is mainly to help understand what you want to get out of this session, then we will look at the current situation and come up with some options and finally a plan. It will last 50 minutes, and I want to make you understand that this is your time. It is confidential and if you feel like you need to take a break at any time just let me know.
		Please have pen and paper with you as we will need to write down some things.
		Before we start, it is important to mention that coaching is about unlocking your potential to maximize your performance, I aim to help you to do that, I am committed to helping you succeed; I will ask questions to help me

understand and support you with your goal. Coaching often involves thinking 'outside of the box,' which sometimes means searching for an answer where first you thought there might be none.

My role as your coach is to be there 100%, to make sure you have an impactful and useful coaching session as possible to enable you to achieve what you want, you have to be ready to take action towards your goal. So unless you have any questions, is it okay if we start?

Yes, I am ready!

| (G) Goal setting | Coach | **Brilliant, let's start with you telling me, what you want to get from this session today?** |
| | Client | Because of the financial difficulties at work, which I told you, I find myself working very long hours but not achieving much that time. I feel like I need a way that I can be more effective in planning my work so that I can get more done in less time if possible. I am spending all day in meetings and spend evenings responding to emails; I feel something has to change because I need to spend more time with my family. |

(Continue)

Coach   Okay, so what do you hope to get from this session today?

Client   I love my job so quitting is not an option, but I think there must be a way that I can enjoy it more and still have time for my family who matters a lot to me. I also need to have a social life which seems to have disappeared since getting this position.

Coach   Okay, what do you aim to get for this session today?

Client   I want to understand how I can manage my time much better and gain a better work-life balance

Coach   Okay, I would like you to tell me that again but as a goal this time… by that I mean you frame it in a way that will help you look forward to the end of the session and see what you hope to achieve. So, if you start with "by the end of the session I…

Client   Okay [silence] ***By the end of this session I will have a plan on how I can manage my time better so that I can achieve more in less time.***

	Coach	Let me repeat what you have said to see if I understand. ***By the end of the session, you will have a plan on how you can manage your time better so that you achieve more in less time?***
	Client	Yes that's right, **by the end of this session I will have a plan on how I can manage my time better so that I can achieve more in less time**
(R) Reality (current situation)	Coach	Fabulous, now that we have our goal. Just write it down on your paper. What would success in that plan look like to you?
	Client	Hmm, I will get to work at 7 am and leave at 5 pm realistically, in that time I would have attended some meeting, written up some paper or report and supported my staff with their needs. Not every day is the same I know, but if I can do this often, then that will be a success to me. [client goes on to explain situations while the coach attentively listens and mirroring the client]

(Continue)

Coach   What is stopping you from doing that?

Client   I don't know [silence by both] maybe there is too much work [Silence again]. I guess there is too much demand on my time.

Coach   What else?

Client   Not sure [silence]

Coach   Who gives you the work?

Client   Well, it's the demand of the organisation and my position. [Silence] there are so many priorities and targets that I need to meet.

Trying to find ways of improving business and making the business profitable again by cutting costs etc.

Coach   On your piece of paper, would you mind drawing a line in the middle, and across on the top, please write down on the top left side a list of tasks in your typical day. On the bottom left, write down the people you encounter in your day. (client writes down the list)

Okay, now from the top list can you think of which three tasks are most critical? i.e., if I do not do them, there will be consequences.

From the list of people, select three people that are most helpful.

Now tell me from those two lists, if you were looking from the outside, What do you have that you're not using?

Client   Trying to find ways of improving business and making the business profitable again by cutting costs.

Coach   Anything else?

Client   Well, the time to get things done?

Coach   What would be helpful to you right now based on the list in front of you? [pause, long silence, giving the client time to think]

Client   [Laughter from the client, still silence from the coach]

Oh, I get it, some of the tasks on this list are more important than other, so I guess I can do them first!

Coach   Great, anything else? What is going on?

(Continue)

	Client	I have too many things to do, but I need to do them.
	Coach	Look again at your paper can you tell me about the top three people you listed and why?
(O) **Options** **[client** **Identifies** **options to** **get them** **to goal]**	Client	[Client explains the list and identifies that some of the people can help by taking on the lesser tasks if she delegates to them.] Oh goodness Eureka! I could ask May, John and Kate to help, in fact, that would be a development opportunity for Kate [smile]
	Coach	Brilliant, you are doing great Marcia, now we need to think about what else you can do. [some questions follow to allow the client to explore all options until comfortable]
	Client	Wow, I know what I am going to do now. I am going to go back and look at all my tasks, see which ones I can allocate to other people. I will also see which meetings I can send someone else to attend and feedback

I could speak my line manager to see if I can get an external consultant to help me draw up the strategy for me. It will free up my time and will help get things done quicker.

(W) Will to do the work to get to goal

Coach   So, of all the options you have listed, which one do you think you can work on over the next week?

[Again some questions and answers including, who the client needs to consider? When will she start? What resources does she need, what help would she need from the coach?]

Marcia, that's great, how do you feel about your plan now?

Client   Happier and more in control

Coach   What commitment on a 1-to-10 scale do you have to take these actions we have agreed?

Client   Eight

Coach   What is stopping it from being a 10?

Client   Well, I am a bit worried that they might make mistakes if I give them the work

(Continue)

Coach	What is the worst that would happen if they made mistakes? [silence, then some questions to explore what would happen if they make mistakes until I find a solution, then the client gives response below or similar]
Client	Well, I guess I would help them, fix it, or they might be okay. They are quite intelligent.
Coach	Great so, now you know there will be no lasting damage, and you can fix the mistakes, and it would be a learning opportunity for them, which would give you a sense of pride when you fix the problem. On a scale of 1 -10 What is your level of commitment to taking these agreed actions?
Client	10!
Coach	Great, now that we have a plan and the will to execute it is a massive 10, when will you complete the tasks? [Here the coach is looking for timeframe commitment, beginning with the end in mind, then asking

several follow up questions to determine the starting point and any milestones, the client wishes to set for herself.]

Client   Oh, maybe next month? I will have made my list and discussed with my manager, then have meetings with the team, in fact, I have a one to one booked for John and Mary which is a great start.

Coach   Wow, that is good, I am so proud of you. When next month? [some good follow up questions to ask are questions such as; who can help you achieve that task? What would you need to have in place? What else? These questions help the client think deeper and come up with other ways, in case the first way does not work]

So how do you feel now?

Client   I feel happy; I feel more in control. I can clearly see how I can free up some time while developing my staff at the same time.

(Continue)

Coach	Fabulous, so now going back to where we started, with the goal you wrote down, how do you feel the session went?
Client	Wow, brilliant, I am going away with a plan as I wanted. I am committed to achieving the result, thank you.
Coach	Oh, look we are just on time, is there anything else I can help you with today?
Client	No, I think we have covered a lot, thank you.
Coach	Okay so we are going to end the session here, but you know that I am reachable by phone or email, if you get stuck and you want to go over something before our next session. Have a productive week. Thank you very much for today, I enjoyed our session. I am looking forward to the next session. Bye for now.

Remember, the client generates the answers for their actions. It is not the job of the coach to advise the client on what to do. I have met people who say they are coaches, although when you listen to them, they play the role of a consultant. I used to be one of those myself.

By nature, we are conditioned to telling others what to do. After all, we were always told what to do by our teachers, parents and even friends. Coaching tends to give the power back to the person. Richard Branson, on one of his quotes, says he employs people who are smarter than him. So, does every great leader. Imagine taking someone who is very educated and has invested in skills only to be told what to do

I have worked with micro-managers in my time; it is not fun at all. They zap the joy out of work. Coaching can help such managers learn new habits and help them develop profitable teams.

CHAPTER SEVEN

Becoming a Coach Manager

It is not always necessary to employ an external coach. Anyone can learn to live their life as a coach to others. We always hear statements such as 'ask more questions, listen more, speak less. All these may sound simplistic, but that is what basic coaching is all about.

In a business setting, try to ask your staff what they think rather than telling them what to do. This can be difficult conditioning if you as a leader are used to give instructions or the staff is used to being told what to do and how to do it.

The easiest way of making this change is to start with self-reflection and self-awareness. This will allow you to become aware of the tendency to tell then you will turn the urge into carefully crafted questions.

To do that, start by searching within yourself. Ask yourself some intense questions about your leadership and each of your roles and areas of responsibility. These questions sample questions only, use them only as a guide. Or you might want to ask different questions altogether. The aim is to help you with self-reflection, which seems to be in short supply when you have a lot of demands on your time. Include you can ask:

1. When am I at my best/worst as parent/employer/ employee/spouse?
2. What are my natural talents?
3. What is the important aspect of my life?

4. What gives me the most energy?
5. What habits can I change now to increase my energy levels even more?
6. What is my passion?
7. Who is my inspiration for my professional and, or personal relationships?
8. Which role models can I follow?
9. What values guide my life and relationships?
10. What core values or principles I am not prepared to violate?
11. What governs me?
12. What affects my self-esteem the most?

Answering the above questions will help you start building yourself awareness which will come in handy when you coach other people.

Coaching Someone Else

Coaching is very much about asking the right questions at the right time. It also has the intuition and ability to ask good follow up questions which will make the client find the answers deep within themselves. The person you are coaching becomes your client, and I will refer to your staff as a client for convenience.

As a coach, you must learn to allow the person you are coaching to think. That means allowing for those silent moments or the *'pregnant pause,' you as a coach has to be comfortable with these moments. The client will expect, you to ask another question or she/he will be processing the last question and digging deeper within for an answer.*

Allowing such moments can yield very big and significant results.

One way of allowing this is for you to count slowly from ten to one internally.

When you coach your staff, you may be confronted with paranoia or resistance. I would suggest that you are transparent. You can tell the person; you are trying out a new way of leading. They will be more open and receptive that way.

Some Great Coaching Questions

A full coaching competency session is beyond this book. You will find that different situations require different questions. *'Go with your gut.' It is always key to be clear about the reason and circumstances in which you are coaching. Try not to complicate the situation. Have fun with your staff. You will get better results from them.*

Over time I have accumulated a list of generally helpful questions to ask. I will share some of those with you. They are not all my original inventions, but I use them in my practice, and I find that they unlock a lot from my client. Remember, it is easier to get someone to be more productive when they feel heard and cared for. These questions go beyond the task at hand alone. Your staff will thank you for showing interest in their life. That will lead to them having a better sense of fulfillment and ownership in their job.

You may be worried that some of the questions will open *'cans of worms' that you may not want to deal with or require a* referral. Your job is, to be honest, and transparent. Do not promise what you cannot deliver but you can make referrals or suggestions for them to explore.

Here are my thirty favourite questions to ask. You might find them helpful to ask your staff:

1. What are you scheduling to create time for work / yourself?
2. What are you working on right now?
3. What are your daily practices?
4. Where are you struggling?
5. What have you done that has helped?
6. What else do you need to create the change, you are desiring?
7. What are the three words that describe your best self?
8. What are the tools you currently use to be the best version of yourself?
9. What are the limiting beliefs you tell yourself?
10. How would you re-phrase those limiting beliefs?
11. What do you do when your best self-doesn't show through?
12. What level of engagement do you have in your life?

13. What area do you need to improve on right now?
14. How important is it to you to improve this area?
15. What personally challenges you to be the best in productivity?
16. What does the first hour of your day look like?
17. How much of your time is each day spent taking care of others or prioritizing other people's needs?
18. What is the impact of that choice?
19. What does it cost you with that choice?
20. What is most important to you now?
21. What will be most important three months from now?
22. What would you do if no one was looking or evaluating (judging) you?
23. What is bringing you the most fulfillment in work life?
24. What new skills would you like to develop?
25. What are your greatest accomplishments in this job (or in the last six months)?
26. What are the biggest stressors in this job (or in the last six months)?
27. What do you do for fun and relaxation?
28. What do you value most?
29. When you feel aligned how do you show up?
30. What three things could you start doing to increase in fulfillment and intention consistently?

The Ultimate Productivity Reading List

1. 101 Coaching Strategies and Techniques (Essential Coaching Skills and Knowledge) by Gladeana McMahon and Anne Archer.

2. Co-Active Coaching, 3rd Edition: Changing Business, Transforming Lives by Henry Kimsey-House et al.

3. Coaching for Performance: The Principles and Practices of Coaching and Leadership (People Skills for Professionals) by John Whitmore

4. Eat That Frog! Get More of the Important Things Done - Today! by Brian Tracy

5. Getting Things Done: The Art of Stress-Free Productivity by David Allen

6. How to be a Productivity Ninja: Worry Less, Achieve More and Love What You Do by Graham Allcott

7. The Five Dysfunctions of a Team: A Leadership Fable by Patrick Lencioni

8. The Productivity Project: Proven Ways to Become More Awesome by Chris Bailey

9. Think and Grow Rich by Napoleon Hill

10. Work Smarter Not Harder: 18 Productivity Tips That Boost Your Work Day Performance Kindle Edition by Timo Kiander

Conclusion

The conclusion to be drawn from the research to develop this book shows evidence that coaching provides benefits to both management and staff within the organisation. Using coaching can help the individuals within the organisation to increase their productivity and general wellbeing leading higher productivity for the organisation.

A coaching programme for the managers can make a valuable contribution towards changing their management styles which can help in challenging hindering beliefs and increasing optimism, assisting with career planning/personal development and improving communication within the organisation and externally.

Organisations that use coaching value their staff, making them feeling empowered and responsible for their achievements, improving individual performance and productivity and motivation. Areas of coaching such as coaching for change and conflict resolution are a good way of keeping staff engaged and reducing conflict and improving co-operation. Managers can use this in managing change and dealing with underperformance. Other ways coaching can help are:

→ Demonstrating a commitment to the staff and improving morale
→ Enabling staff to maximize the benefit they receive from other training
→ Increasing job satisfaction
→ Improving the work-life balance and reduce stress

It is preferable to other methods of training such as in-house or bespoke management development, e-learning programmes and shadowing or secondments, as it is targeted rather than generic. Coaching allows individuals to focus on their needs by setting their goals, assessing their current situation, identifying best practice, considering and selecting strategies and options. Putting these into practice by deciding how who, and when to progress. It promotes ownership, enabling the managers to assess their strengths and weaknesses and make decisions to achieve objectives. As a supportive activity focusing on the individual, it can be flexible regarding delivering the one to one coaching as required. However, it has not been possible at this stage to establish if the organisations that provide coaching for their staff are better than those that do not. There is not enough evidence at present to back up this theory. More work is needed to establish some facts over time. This topic has the potential for a very interesting Ph.D. research topic certainly worth considering.

Organisations are encouraged to offer to coach their staff, the evidence of the benefits is overwhelming.

Check Out More of My Books

Solo Authorship

These are books I have written alone. I wrote and published my first book in March 2017. The book you are reading is my third book, and I have one or two more coming within the next 12 months. The books are available on Amazon and other distributors. You can also order them directly through the Diverse Cultures Publishing Website at www.diverse-cultures.co.uk

1. **The Serious Player's Decisive Business Start-up Guide:** How to Set Up Your Business in 4 Easy-to-Follow Steps, Published in March 2017.

2. **Pushing Through Fear, Stereotypes, and Imperfections:** How to COACH Yourself Through

> Life's CHALLENGES and Boost Your MENTAL
> HEALTH
>
> 3. **PROFITABLE TEAMS:** The Art of Increasing
>   Productivity and Profits Through Coaching.

Books Co-authored with Other People

In 2009 I was asked by a lady in the USA called Linda
Ellis-Eastman to co-author a chapter in one of her books.
So I did, between 2009 and 2013 I co-authored chapters
in three of her books. I did not think much about what
I was doing then, apart from the fact that I was sharing
what I knew.

Through that process, I was invited to speak at some
events, including one that was close to my heart as I pre-
sented the Perfect Migrant at the International Metrop-
olis Conference at The Hague. I made efforts to keep
the momentum going, but it was not until I decided to
start helping other people within my circle to write that
I realised the power that writing has. So when I left my
Corporate Job in February 2017, I set out to start writing and publishing in addition to my coaching business.
The last year (as we are now in February 2018) has been
amazing. It has been a year of growth for me, but it has
also been a great help to the people that have trusted me
with their stories and co-authored chapters in my books.
By June 2018 we will publish the first three co-authored

books. Here are the three titles I co-authored with Ms. Linda Ellis-Eastman founder of PWN books and the last three are the ones that we are releasing through my company Diverse Cultures Publishing.

I hope you will get the opportunity to read them. It is also my hope that soon I will be co-authoring with you.

1. **How to Break the Glass Ceiling without Using a Hammer** (Chapter - Home Away from Home). 15 Dec 2010. Published by PWN Books, USA

2. **Madam CEO: How to Think and Act Like a Chief Executive** (Chapter - Face the Fear and Do It Anyway: Handling Transition and Change). 8 December 2011. Published by PWN Books, USA

3. **What's the Difference? Embracing Diversity & Inclusivity** (Chapter - Succeeding in a World with Diverse Cultures). 1 Sep 2013. Published by PWN Books, USA

4. **Celebrating Diversity:** Sharing Positive Stories of Migration from Around the World. - May 2018, Published by Diverse Cultures Publishing, UK.

5. **The Power of the Diasporan African Woman:** Stories of Strength and Positivity - June 2018. Published by Diverse Cultures Publishing, UK

6. **Leading:** How to Be Your Own Boss! - July 2018. Published by Diverse Cultures Publishing. UK

Can We Work Together Next?

I humbly and excitedly invite you to become an author with us or to write your next book with us.

Diverse Cultures Publishing will be releasing more books co-authored by different people from around the world. We would love you to be part of the revolution in writing through collaboration. The investment you will make to become a co-author will offer you so much value for money.

For details on how it works go to www.diverse-cultures.co.uk.

Alternatively, email us to arrange a call at publishing@diverse-cultures.co.uk.

Acknowledgment

This book comes from the heart; it is an accumulation of the lessons I have learned from many great teachers, coaches, and clients who I have had the great opportunity of working with and have paved the way to be the best that I have always aspired to be. I am still growing, and I believe I will meet many more great people in my professional journey as a productivity and high-performance coach. To all the people that have influenced me, too many to mention. I say wholeheartedly thank you for being you and for helping me.

This work would not have been possible without some very remarkable people in my life and those I have met along my journey of growth.

First and foremost, we all have a belief of a superpower somewhere that resides upon us. As a Christian, I thank God for His wisdom and unfailing love upon me and my loved ones. I am always grateful that I am still in this world to share what I know and to serve to the best of my ability.

I would like to thank the following pillars in my life:

My husband, Ali Abdoul, a man of few words and a pillar that I can lean on in my times of weakness and celebrate within happy moments. *Je t'aime mon chéri*, my French Comorian rare gem.

My children; Child Number One and Child Number Two: Ngosa Kambashi aka the *'Boss Sister'* and Razina Ngweshe Kambashi aka the *'Best Friend' to my little ones*. You have grown to be my best friends, I love you and thank you for your support with this book and for believing in my crazy dreams. My 'forensic psychologist' Ngosa, you are a force to reckon with, very caring, you are there for me always asking if I am okay, you too have grown to be my best friend. Thanks for the glasses of wine.

Ngweshe you are such an amazing young lady, quietly a problem solver and always willing to listen to my ideas, and thanks for the overflowing cups of tea through my writing.

Child Number Three Naila Abdoul and Child Number Four Iman Abdoul. My Munchkins, you two bring so much joy to my life, there is no dull moment with you, mummy loves you.

To a very special lady, Ms. Thandi Haruperi, you listened to me in 2016 and pushed me to follow my dreams and to write a book. Thank you, sis. We need more people like you in the world.

To two companies that have helped me shape my business, Peter Thomson International (UK) and the Brendon Burchard Group (USA). You are all amazing, thank you for welcoming me into your professional families.

To all my business associates, my coaches, my mentors and my clients, To everyone in this category, I would not run my businesses without all of you guys. Thank you to all the authors that I have quoted in this book. Your work has seen me here.

To my National Health Service (NHS) colleagues, thanks for the experience.

There are a lot more people I would love to mention, but all I can say to everyone who has contributed to my life, my fans and followers on social media too:

Thank you! I honour you.

What Next for You?

Firstly, thanks a million for taking time to read my book. Your reviews are important to me, and as they say, there is no shame in asking for help. So here is my request. If you enjoyed this book and learned something from it, you can help me in one or more of the following ways:

→ Go online, at www.amazon.co.uk or my website www.aminachitembo.com, write a kind review.

→ Check out our other books at www.diverse-cultures. co.uk

→ Let us connect on Social Media and share more of what we know my handle is @aminachitembo in some cases its @aminachitembo1.

→ Attend one of my training or seminars

→ Be the happily Imperfect Leader, be brave and blast any fears of trying something new.

→ Email me if I can be of any help with your coaching or someone you know amina@diverse-cultures .com. I do reply directly.

→ Get a copy of this book as a gift to your friend or family.

→ Continue to grow to the next level of your life and build the happy life and success you want. Join one of my coaching programmes at www.aminachitembo .com

THANK YOU FOR YOUR SUPPORT.

About the Author

Amina Chitembo is a UK based British/Zambian multi-award-winning Entrepreneur, Author, Speaker, Trainer, and Business High-Performance Coach. **She is the go-to coach for senior executives, leadership teams, and their staff.**

She consults, and trains integrated organisations and businesses, helping people to increase resilience, productivity, and profitability while maintaining outstanding levels of high-performance and thereby improving mental health, wellbeing and financial stability in the workplace.

As an inspirational speaker, Amina champions **Leadership: The Link between Productivity, Financial Stability and Mental Health in the Workplace.** She works internationally with leaders who juggle huge responsibilities of leading others, staying on top of business demands and profitability even in challenging times. After overcoming many difficulties to become a leader herself, she helps people to increase personal and professional success by challenging fears, stereotypes and defying imperfections, thereby reducing mental health issues.

FREE ONLINE TOOLS

Get some productivity tools from other thought leaders and me, coaches and authors who have allowed me to share theirs at:

https://www.aminachitembo.com/p/productivity-tools

I will see you there.

—Amina.

Bibliography

CIPD. (2004). *Coaching and buying coaching services.*

Hailey, B. a. (2004). *Exploring Strategic Change.* Prentice Hall.

Learning Partnership Consultancy. (2010). *Building a business case for coaching white paper.*

Parsole, E. (1999). *The Manager as a Coach and Mentor.* CIPD.

Stanford University and Miles Group. (2013). *Executive Coaching Survey.*

Lassiter, D. (2004). The Business Case for Coaching. Leadership Advantage Newsletter.

Anderson, M.C., Frankovelgia, C. & Hernez-Broome. G. (2008). *Creating coaching cultures. What business leaders expect and strategies to get there.* Greensboro, North Carolina: Center for Creative Leadership.

Chartered Institute of Personnel and Development (2010). *Learning and talent development. Annual survey 2010.* London: CIPD.

Chartered Institute of Personnel and Development (2009).*Taking the temperature of coaching: coaching summer survey.* London: CIPD.

http://www.coachingnetwork.org.uk/resourcecentre/ whatarecoachingandmentoring.htm

Angela Armstrong: Performance | Leadership | Results . . ." Insert Name of Site in Italics. N.p., n.d. Web. 04 Oct. 2016 <http://www.angelaarmstrong.com/coaching>.

Building a business case for coaching A guide for human . . ." Insert Name of Site in Italics. N.p., n.d. Web. 04 Oct. 2016 <http://www.lcp.org.uk/images/ LCP_%20Building_a_Business_Case_for_Coaching_2010.p>.

Results You Get with Executive Coaching http://www. monarch-janus.com/mja-executive-coaching-results. html

A little gem for futuristic leaders and business owners who want to discover how coaching can exponentially increase your productivity and profitability and help you build expert teams.

In **Profitable Teams: The Art of Increasing Productivity and Profits Through Coaching**. The author, Amina Chitembo, explores and simplifies the understanding of how coaching can help anyone who wants to take their business or organisation to that next level of productivity leveraging the best assets.

Promoting Easy and Inclusive Reading.